BLUE BANNER
BIOGRAPHY

Abby
WAMBACH

John Bankston

Mitchell Lane
PUBLISHERS
P.O. Box 196
Hockessin, Delaware 19707
Visit us on the web: www.mitchelllane.com
Comments? Email us: mitchelllane@mitchelllane.com

Mitchell Lane
PUBLISHERS

Printing   2   3   4   5   6   7   8   9

Blue Banner Biographies

Abby Wambach	Gwen Stefani	Mary-Kate and Ashley Olsen
Adele	Ice Cube	Megan Fox
Alicia Keys	Ja Rule	Miguel Tejada
Allen Iverson	Jamie Foxx	Mike Trout
Ashanti	Jay-Z	Nancy Pelosi
Ashlee Simpson	Jennifer Hudson	Natasha Bedingfield
Ashton Kutcher	Jennifer Lopez	Nicki Minaj
Avril Lavigne	Jessica Simpson	One Direction
Blake Lively	J. K. Rowling	Orianthi
Bow Wow	John Legend	Orlando Bloom
Brett Favre	Justin Berfield	P. Diddy
Britney Spears	Justin Timberlake	Peyton Manning
Bruno Mars	Kanye West	Prince William
CC Sabathia	Kate Hudson	Queen Latifah
Carrie Underwood	Katy Perry	Robert Downey Jr.
Chris Brown	Keith Urban	Ron Howard
Chris Daughtry	Kelly Clarkson	Sean Kingston
Christina Aguilera	Kenny Chesney	Shakira
Clay Aiken	Ke$ha	Shia LaBeouf
Cole Hamels	Kevin Durant	Shontelle Layne
Condoleezza Rice	Kristen Stewart	Soulja Boy Tell 'Em
Corbin Bleu	Lady Gaga	Stephenie Meyer
Daniel Radcliffe	Lance Armstrong	Taylor Swift
David Ortiz	Leona Lewis	T.I.
David Wright	Lionel Messi	Timbaland
Derek Jeter	Lindsay Lohan	Tim McGraw
Drew Brees	LL Cool J	Tim Tebow
Eminem	Ludacris	Toby Keith
Eve	Mariah Carey	Usher
Fergie	Mario	Vanessa Anne Hudgens
Flo Rida	Mary J. Blige	Will.i.am
		Zac Efron

Library of Congress Cataloging-in-Publication Data
Bankston, John, 1974-
 Abby Wambach / by John Bankston.
     pages cm. -- (Blue banner biographies)
 Includes bibliographical references and index.
 ISBN 978-1-61228-465-1 (library bound)
 1. Wambach, Abby, 1980---Juvenile literature. 2. Women soccer players--United States--Biography--Juvenile literature. 3. Soccer players--United States--Biography--Juvenile literature. I. Title.
 GV942.7.W36B36 2014
 796.334092--dc23
 [B]
                                                                    2013023036
 eBook ISBN: 9781612285221

ABOUT THE AUTHOR: Born in Boston, Massachusetts, John Bankston began writing articles while still a teenager. Since then, over two hundred of his articles have been published in magazines and newspapers across the country, including travel articles in *The Tallahassee Democrat, The Orlando Sentinel* and *The Tallahassean*. He is the author of over sixty biographies for young adults, including works on Alexander the Great, scientist Stephen Hawking, author F. Scott Fitzgerald, and actor Jodi Foster.

PUBLISHER'S NOTE: The following story has been thoroughly researched, and to the best of our knowledge represents a true story. While every possible effort has been made to ensure accuracy, the publisher will not assume liability for damages caused by inaccuracies in the data and makes no warranty on the accuracy of the information contained herein. This story has not been authorized or endorsed by Abby Wambach.

Blue Banner Biography

On August 21, 2008 the U.S. Olympic team celebrates their overtime victory against Brazil in the gold medal match. Team member Abby Wambach was home with an injury.

A Bad Break

*A*bby Wambach's U.S. Women's National Soccer Team won the gold medal at the 2008 Olympics in Beijing, China, as they defeated Brazil 1–0. Victory for the United States arrived with a left-footed kick into the goal delivered by Carli Lloyd during overtime. Millions of people celebrated the triumph. It was the culmination of a challenging season, the result that Abby's team had worked toward for years.

Abby wasn't on the field. She didn't play a single minute of the Olympic soccer tournament. In fact, she wasn't even in China. About a month and a half earlier, on July 2, she had almost reached a milestone when she scored her 99th international goal for the U.S. national team. The 100th seemed like it was right around the corner.

On July 16th, Abby was playing in San Diego during the team's final pre-Olympic match. Late in the first half, she ran at full speed toward Brazil's goal and took her shot. As the ball sailed away, she collided with Brazilian defender Andreia Rosa. Abby flew into the air, helicoptered, and crashed to the ground. The collision shattered two bones in her left leg.

To many people, Abby was the best player on the U.S. team and the gruesome injury appeared to shatter the chances of the U.S. to win the gold medal. Abby disagreed with this belief. "Obviously, it's devastating, but above everything else, I'm only one player, and you can never win a championship with just one player," she said in a statement soon after the game in which she was injured. "I have the utmost confidence in this team bringing home the gold."

Moments after the U.S. team justified Abby's confidence in them and brought home the gold medal, the equipment manager called Abby and then set the phone down in the locker room. Abby listened from thousands of miles away to her excited teammates.

Although she was thrilled, her pain was greater than a broken leg. "There were some tears of joy and obviously

Taken out of the game by Brazilian Andreia Rosa, Abby Wambach lies on the field in agony. She suffered a broken left tibia and fibula.

some tears of devastation that I wasn't there to be a part of it," she admitted to *USA Today* several years later.

Abby was 28, a power forward who was traveling the world and getting paid to do the thing she loved best. Just four years earlier, she'd helped her team win the gold medal at the Athens Olympics.

Now Abby should have been at the peak of her career. Instead, her body was a damaged mess of injuries. She'd already suffered concussions and a torn Achilles tendon. The broken leg would take months to heal. Even then, there was no guarantee she'd recover.

In Athens, Greece members of the U.S. Olympic Team pose following their gold medal victory over Brazil in 2004.

History repeats itself as four years later, the team scores another gold medal victory against Brazil at the Beijing Olympics in 2008.

U.S. soccer fans wondered if she'd ever send a ball into the net for her 100th international goal. "I was heartbroken," she told *USA Today*. "I think I was mad at the game, because I thought that I had worked hard enough and I had done all the things that I needed to give me that chance."

The hard work had begun more than 20 years earlier. That was even before Abby had reached elementary school age, with painful lessons learned at the hands of four older brothers in a family of competitive athletes.

CHAPTER 2

The Natural

South of Lake Ontario, the Genesee River passes by New York towns and cities that are dependent on its water. At one point, they used it not just for drinking, but also for power and farming. Three large waterfalls called cataracts sliced into land which became the city of Rochester. Powered by the rushing water, sawmills and flour mills flourished. When flour production eventually moved west and the flour mills disappeared, the city became a garden center. Rochester even changed its nickname from "Flour City" to "Flower City."

The Wambach family called Rochester home for generations. Pete and Judy Wambach ran a local garden center, raising their family in Pittsford—a comfortable suburb eight miles from the city center.

Mary Abigail Wambach was born on June 2, 1980. Her parents already had six children—two other girls and four boys.

Growing up with four older brothers, Abby had a rough-and-tumble childhood. Her brothers once hung her from a doorknob by her underwear. She remembers kicking the whole time. Her strong legs and willingness to fight even when she was outmatched would later serve her well. As the youngest of seven kids, she constantly had to struggle to get her family's attention.

One day, her older sister Beth came home with a book from the library. She hoped the book would help her learn how to play soccer. She got Abby to help her learn some of the moves that the book illustrated. Abby soon revealed that she had a talent for the sport.

In Abby's first three recreational soccer games, she scored 27 goals. Her natural ability surpassed the other players her age. She appeared to be unstoppable.

When she was five years old, Abby joined a youth recreational league. Over the course of three games, Abby scored 27 goals. Her natural ability surpassed the other players her age. She appeared to be unstoppable.

Her athletic gifts seemed natural. At home, she was surrounded by athletes. Besides her siblings, her father had been a wrestler and a runner. And her mother helped encourage physical fitness. As Abby explained to the *New York Times*, "My mom would literally lock us out of the house and say 'go play.' We wouldn't be able to come in, not even to pee. I feel like I was kind of bred in some ways to do what I do now."

Soccer players wear very little protective equipment. Given a choice between her body and the goal, Abby Wambach chose the goal. When people call her fearless, it may be due less to the training she got on the soccer field than those early days outside the Wambach home when her brothers played street hockey in the confines of their neighborhood cul-de-sac. After dressing Abby in ill-fitting pads, they used her as a goalie. "I was almost bred to be an athlete," she said to the *New York Post*. "The youngest of seven, thrown into a hockey goal at a young age and told to stay there... my competitiveness was taught to me at a very young age."

Judy Wambach cheers her daughter Abby after a soccer match against South Korea held at Red Bull arena in Harrison, New Jersey.

Playing girls' soccer was easy compared to defending herself against slap shots from older boys. "Boys aren't going to let you win, no matter what," she told the *New York Times*. "I had to learn to use my body because the boys were stronger than I was."

In the United States soccer is by far the most popular sport for women and girls, with some eight million players. Still, local coaches felt she would be better matched with boys her own age than with girls. When she was 9, the league moved her from the girls team to the boys. The change didn't affect her goal-scoring ability. "That was probably one of the most influential things in terms of my career," she explained on her video blog. "Just having that mentality of going into a game, no matter who you're gonna go up against— whether it's a boy, a strong woman, tall, short, fast—the ability to switch your mindset to just play your own game and play the best that you can play, and almost playing fearless and I think that's one major attribute that I got from playing with the boys."

> *In the United States soccer is by far the most popular sport for women and girls, with some eight million players.*

Breaking Records

*P*laying against both boys and girls, Abby as a preteen was already honing the skills she'd need as a pro soccer player. By the time she was 11, Abby had begun "heading" the ball. This is a difficult and potentially dangerous move. The player must keep her upper body arched with her shoulders squared to the target, her chest and neck snapping forward so that she can make contact with the ball at her hairline.

The risks are huge. While heading a ball, Abby could collide with another player or even a goalpost. Hitting the ball incorrectly can also cause an injury. To head the ball, therefore, Abby had to be fearless. It was something she learned playing with her brothers. She believed that no matter if she was hurt or how badly she lost, she would win the next time she played with them.

One of Abby's coaches as an adult, Jim Gabarra, explained to the *New York Times* what a player needs to successfully head the ball. "A lot of it is determination and will—I don't care who is in the way. Some players have that fear, 'Is someone going to hit me in the air? Is the

Abby strikes a "header" against Japan on August 9, 2012 during the Olympic women's soccer final in London, England.

goalkeeper going to punch me in the head? Will I land funny?'"

Over the course of her career, Abby Wambach would score goals by hitting the ball off her ear, the back of her head, her hip, and even her back. As a preteen, however, she used heading to move the ball down the field, popping it over the heads of surprised defenders and then running around them.

At Our Lady of Mercy High School, Abby was a starter during all four years she played on the varsity team. During that time, she scored 142 goals, including 34 in her final year in 1997. Besides playing for her high school team, she was captain for the Rochester Spirit, a club team. In 1996, she joined the Olympic Development Team. The next year she traveled to Beijing, joining the first U.S. youth soccer team to compete in China.

In 1997, she was named the National Soccer Coaches Association of America (NSCAA) Regional player of the year and State of New York player of the year.

In 1997, she was named the National Soccer Coaches Association of America (NSCAA) Regional player of the year and State of New York player of the year. Her achievements were also noticed far away from Rochester. Across the country, the NSCAA ranks high school soccer players. In 1996 and 1997 they chose Abby as a High School All-American and in 1997 the National Player of the Year. *USA Today* named her as one of the country's top ten recruits, while *Parade Magazine* named her to its High School All-American Soccer Team.

A number of colleges with top-ranked soccer programs wanted Abby to play for their teams. The University of California at Los Angeles (UCLA), the University of North Carolina, the University of Virginia, and George Mason University—which is located in Virginia, not far from the national capital of Washington, D.C.—

> Abby later told the SEC Digital Network she didn't want to join a team that had already won the national championship. Instead, she wanted to be a part of a team on its way up.

offered her full scholarships, which would include tuition and room and board. Instead she chose the University of Florida at Gainesville.

Abby later told the SEC Digital Network she didn't want to join a team that had already won the national championship. Instead, she wanted to be a part of a team on its way up. "I wanted to be part of something new, something fresh and a team that beat a dynasty like UNC [University of North Carolina]," she explained. "I thought my best chance of doing that was at the University of Florida." In 1998, she left Rochester for college in Florida, hoping to join a team that might go all the way.

Goal!

As a freshman playing for the University of Florida Gators, Abby knew that she might be overshadowed by the team's more experienced players. "There were so many seniors on that team that had a personal hand in creating and developing the program themselves," she told SEC Digital. "For me, the family environment and the mentality of playing for your teammates fit in with my personal values. It wasn't like the seniors were too good for the freshmen. They really accepted us and knew that they needed us to win."

She quickly adapted to playing at the college level. She started all of the 26 games she played as a freshman, and her 19 goals were second-highest on the team. She recorded her first hat trick—scoring three goals in a single game—during a match against Kentucky while leading her team to a 3-0 victory. By the end of the season, she was earning accolades that usually went to older college players, including being named to the NSCAA All-Southeast Region First Team.

Much more important, the Gators won the National Collegiate Athletic Association (NCAA) championship for the first time. Wambach told SEC Digital that winning the 1998 National Championship "was one of the best things to ever happen to me. It was not only exciting and exhilarating, but it was also really satisfying and it really fulfilled so many different things for me."

Over the course of four years playing for the Gators, Wambach broke a number of school records—including assists, game-winning goals, and hat tricks. She also had a record-breaking 241 points. By the end of her career at Florida, she was the school's all-time leader in goals scored and game-winning goals. Those records have yet to be broken.

> By the end of her career at Florida, she was the school's all-time leader in goals scored and game-winning goals. Those records have yet to be broken.

Abby believes that playing for the University of Florida was vital to her development as a player. On her website, AbbyWambach.com, she was asked about people who helped her advance in her career. She named her University of Florida trainer, Randy Bower, along with Santa Clara University soccer coach Jerry Smith, who coached her on the Under-21 National Team. "These people gave me the tools to be successful," she explained. "It was then up to me, because at some point you have to accept the information and all the help you're getting from the outside world and internalize it and put it into a product on the field."

It was Smith, the husband of soccer star Brandi Chastain (one of Abby's role models), who changed the course of her life. He told her he thought she could play for the Women's National Team. She believed him. She knew the chance of being a professional soccer player in the U.S. was slim, but she couldn't imagine doing anything else.

"I didn't realize until late in my college career that it was actually something I could do after college, maybe for a living and as a career," she explained on her website. "Even then, you still had to be the best in the world." Abby didn't know if she was that good, but there was only one way to find out. In 2001, she tried out for the team.

"I believe in my heart that everybody has something that they have to offer, and that they are brilliant at," she said on her website. "It's a journey of life to find that brilliance and to be able to excel at it."

To excel, Abby needed to compete against the best players in the world. To do that, she joined the U.S. Women's National Team in 2001. The National Team competes in both the World Cup and the Olympics. They had won the World Cup in 1991 and 1999, as well as the gold medal at the 1996 Olympics.

Abby did not just play for the National Team. In 2002, she tried out for the Women's United Soccer Association (WUSA), a professional league. She was chosen by the Washington Freedom and was the second player chosen overall. She would play for both the National Team and Washington Freedom for much of the decade.

One reason women's soccer was so successful is that soccer and basketball are the only professional sports available for women. Standing 5 feet, 10 inches tall, Abby told *Muscle & Fitness/Hers* that, "I get asked the basketball question constantly. If it's not basketball, it's volleyball. People think I'm lying when I tell them I play soccer."

On September 16, 2008, NBA Phoenix Suns player Stave Nash talks to (from left to right) Washington Freedom head coach Jim Gabarra and players Cat Whitehall and Abby Wambach.

Still, the skills she'd acquired as a high school basketball player helped her succeed as a professional soccer player. She had learned to track the path of the ball so she would be able to rebound after a missed shot. "I have a unique ability to predict the flight of the ball," she told the *New York Times.*

The skills she brought to the game quickly revealed themselves. On the Washington Freedom, she was able to work with her idol, Mia Hamm. Now retired, Hamm was a founding member of the Freedom and like Abby a high-scoring forward. When Hamm retired in 2004, she held the record for international goals, with 158.

Abby thrived under Hamm's direction. At the end of the season, she was named WUSA Rookie of the Year. In

2003, Hamm and Abby teamed up for 66 combined goals as the Freedom won the league title.

The next year, Abby enjoyed a similar success with the Women's National Team. That January, she joined 27 other players at the pre-Olympic training camp in Carson, California. To prepare for the Olympics, they would devote two hours on the field three days a week, along with three weight training sessions. Because most soccer players run five miles over the course of a game, they were expected to be able to sprint, stop, turn and sprint again for over an hour and a half. As Abby explained in *Muscle & Fitness/Hers* that year, "The mentality of the U.S. Women's National Team is that we're the fittest team in the world. When we're on our own, it's each player's responsibility to stay in excellent shape."

The training paid off when the team competed at the summer Olympics in Athens, Greece. Abby scored four goals and notched one assist. She saved her best for the final game against Brazil. With the teams tied 1–1 at the end of regulation time, the game went into overtime. At the 112th minute, Abby headed the ball off a Brazilian defender and into the net. The U.S. women defeated Brazil 2-1. "It's a fabulous way to win an Olympic gold medal," Abby told the *Washington Post*.

Over the next four years, she started nearly every game the U.S. National Team played. She felt well prepared for the 2008 Summer Olympics. But when her leg was broken the month before the Games, she worried that her career could be over.

Following a 5-0 rout against Korea on June 20, 2013 Abby Wambach is doused in celebration — both of the victory and of her breaking Mia Hamm's all-time international scoring record

Best in the World

After suffering the injury, Abby limped back to Thousand Islands, New York and one of the islands that gave the rustic retreat its name. The scenic spot offered everything Abby needed—except for a television. To watch the Olympics, Abby traveled across Lake Ontario to the mainland. She watched her team's victory over Japan inside the Canadian home of someone she'd never met before. "It's in the middle of nowhere, and I'm literally sitting in this stranger's home watching the game," she remembered in *USA Today*.

After her team's victory, Abby worked hard to recover from her injury. It would take her a year to reach the milestone that had been interrupted by her broken leg. In the summer of 2009, she was playing in her second international game since recovering from the injury. The match, which was against the Canadian National Team, was in Rochester, New York. Abby scored late in the game in a 1–0 win to notch her 100th international goal. She admitted to the Associated Press that "There's nothing more you can ask for than play in front of your home crowd and come through with a milestone like I did today. I couldn't dream of a more picture perfect ending." She added to *USA Today* that, "I was just like, 'OK, now it's over. It's in my past. I can move on.'" Moving on for Abby meant winning the title that had eluded her and the U.S. Women's National Team in 2003 and 2007—the World Cup.

"I would give up every goal I've scored to win this World Cup," she told the *New York Times* before the tournament started. Her ability to head the ball into the goal came into play when the U.S. met Brazil in the quarterfinal match. With less than two minutes remaining, Brazil had a 2–1 lead and the U.S. team seemed destined to lose, which would have been its earliest exit in World Cup play. After stealing the ball deep in their own end, the U.S. hurried the ball downfield. Megan Rapinoe sent a high arching pass toward the goal. Abby rose high into the air and headed the

During the World Cup quarterfinal match against Brazil in Dresden, Germany, Abby Wambach heads the ball into the goal with seconds remaining to tie the match despite the best efforts of the Brazilian goalie and a defender.

ball into the goal. "Abby Wambach has saved the U.S. side in this World Cup," the television announcer screamed. He wasn't the only one screaming. Abby let out a scream of triumph of her own and slid into the corner, where her jubilant teammates mobbed her. It was the latest-ever goal in World Cup history. With the score now tied, the U.S. won on penalty kicks.

Her heroics weren't over. With the score tied at 1–1 late in the semi-final game against France, Abby watched the French defender and realized she was "face marking." Instead of watching both the ball and the player, the defender was focused on Abby. "She had no idea where the ball was," Abby told the *New York Times*.

Using that advantage, Abby told teammate Lauren Cheney to float the ball toward the back post. As Cheney made the corner kick, Abby pushed past the defender.

During the World Cup semifinal match against France on July 13, 2011, Abby Wambach scores the winning goal.

When the ball arrived, she headed it into the goal before crashing into the goalpost.

In the championship game against Japan, Abby seemed like she would once again be the hero. She headed in yet another goal midway through the overtime period. But a defensive lapse with three minutes remaining allowed the Japanese to tie the game at 2–2 and then win the game on penalty kicks.

Abby and the rest of team hoped to find redemption when they faced Japan again in the 2012 London Olympics. As teammate midfielder Megan Rapinoe told *USA Today*, "They snatched our dream."

Four years after Abby's injury, she ached for what she had missed when a team member referenced the game in London that led up to the 2008 Olympics. "Do you remember when we were here and did this?" Wambach remembered in *USA Today*. She admits, "I don't have the heart to be hard on them. I know they forget as easily as I might with someone else."

Although Abby did not score in her team's 2-0 victory over Japan, she was noticed for scoring the second goal against Colombia after being hit in the eye by an opposing player. In January 2013, Abby was named the 2012 FIFA Women's World Player of the Year. Mia Hamm was the only other American woman to win the award, in 2001 and 2002. On US Soccer.com, Abby said "I'm very, very surprised. Individual honors only happen if you have great teams and great people who have given you the chance to be here... I don't think of myself as the best player in the world, just a player who plays on the best team in the world."

Later that year, Abby made a strong case for being the best player in the world. In a game against South Korea on June 20 in Harrison, New Jersey, Abby scored her 158th international goal — her second of the game — to tie her with Mia Hamm for the all-time lead. Ten minutes later, she headed in a corner kick from Megan Rapinoe to set a new record. Just before the end of the first half, Abby knifed between two defenders to score yet again on a crossing pass from Alex Morgan to finish the evening with a grand total of 160 goals. Of that total, 69 have been headers.

Abby was characteristically modest about her feat. "I'm so thankful [that] my teammates were trying to get me those goals," she said in a U.S. Soccer Federation press release. "I can't thank them enough. As a competitor you want to be done with the things that put me at the forefront of conversations. This team is too good to be talking about one person."

"I'm just so proud of her," Hamm added to Associated Press sportswriter Tom Canavan. "Just watching those four goals, that's what she is all about. She fights for the ball, she's courageous and she never gives up. Her strength and perseverance is what makes her so great and it's what defenders and opposing teams fear."

"A hundred and sixty and counting," said the television announcer as Abby hammered home her final goal of the evening. Along with everyone who follows soccer, he clearly expects that Abby will score many more goals before her stellar career is over. Yet for Abby, the most important part of her legacy will be the Olympic gold medals and World Cup titles she helps the U.S. women's team to win. "It's not about the individual," she told USA Today. "It never has been and it never will be."

1980 Mary Abigail Wambach is born on June 2 in Rochester, New York to Pete and Judy Wambach.

1984 Begins playing youth soccer and scores 27 goals in her first three games.

1994 Abby begins playing varsity soccer and basketball for Our Lady of Mercy High School in Rochester; she is eventually named All-Greater Rochester Player of the Year three years in a row in both sports.

1997 The National Soccer Coaches of America names Abby the National Player of the year.

1998 Enters the University of Florida, where she helps the Gators win the NCAA National Championship that year and eventually sets several records.

2001 Joins the U.S. Women's National Team.

2002 Is chosen second in the Women's United Soccer Association (WUSA) draft by the Washington Freedom.

2003 Playing alongside star forward Mia Hamm, Wambach helps the Freedom win the league title.

2003 Is named U.S. Soccer's Female Athlete of the Year and receives the same honor the following year.

2004 Abby scores four goals as the U.S. team wins the gold medal at the Olympic Games in Athens, Greece.

2007 During the World Cup, Abby scores six goals in six matches despite colliding with a North Korean player in the tournament's first match and receiving 11 stitches; the U.S. team finishes third.

2008 During a pre-Olympic match, Abby breaks two bones in her leg after colliding with an opposing player and misses the Olympics.

2009 Abby scores her 100th international goal in a match against Canada played in Rochester, New York.

2011 Abby scores four goals in the World Cup but U.S. women lose to Japan on penalty kicks in the final game.

2012 Abby is named co-captain of the U.S. Women's Olympic team, which wins the gold medal in London as Abby scores five goals.

2013 Abby is named the FIFA Women's World Player of the Year; Abby breaks Mia Hamm's all-time international scoring record with four goals against South Korea to bring her total to 160.

CAREER STATS

World Cup

Year	MP	GS
2003	6	3
2007	6	6
2011	6	4
Total	18	13

Olympics

Year	MP	GS
2004	5	4
2012	6	5
Total	11	9

All Others

Year	MP	GS
2001	1	0
2002	7	5
2003	8	6
2004	28	27
2005	8	4
2006	21	17
2007	15	14
2008	22	13
2009	4	2
2010	18	16
2011	11	4
2012	26	22
2013 (as of 6/20)	9	8
Total	178	138

Grand Total	MP	GS
As of 6/20/13	207	160

MP = Matches Played, GS = Goals Scored

FURTHER READING

Further Reading

Arnold, Caroline. *Soccer: From Neighborhood Play to the World Cup*. New York: Franklin Watts, 1991.

Gifford, Clive. *Soccer*. New York: PowerKids Press, 2009.

Hornby, Hugh, and Andy Crawford. *Soccer*. New York: Dorling Kindersley, 2000.

Kennedy, Mike. *Soccer*. New York: Children's Press, 2002.

Orr, Tamra. *Abby Wambach*. Hockessin, Del.: Mitchell Lane Publishers, 2008.

Shea, Therese. *Soccer Stars*. New York: Children's Press, 2007.

Stewart, Mark, and Mike Kennedy. *Goal: the Fire and Fury of Soccer's Greatest Moments*. Minneapolis: Millbrook Press, 2010.

Works Consulted

"Abby Wambach Gets 100th Goal in U.S. Win Over Canada." Associated Press. July 19, 2009.

Klemko, Robert. "USA, Japan Respectful Rivals in Soccer Final," *USA Today*. August 9, 2012.

Lewis, Brian. "Abby's Long Road, Wambach Has Come Too Far Not to Win," *New York Post*. July 15, 2011.

Longman, Jere. "Wambach Breaks Leg in Exhibition," *New York Times*, July 17, 2008.

"Playing Head Games," *New York Times*. July 17, 2011.

McDowell, Dimity. "Scoring Machine: Soccer Player Abby Wambach is Going for the Gold." *Joe Weider's Muscle and Fitness/Hers*, May, 2004, p. 30.

Michaelis, Vicki. "After Bad Break, Wambach returns to form," *USA Today*. June 30, 2010.

Svrluga, Barry. "U.S. Women Win Soccer Gold Medal," *Washington Post*. August 27, 2004.

"U.S. Team Star Abby Wambach Leaves Her Portland Home to Anchor New York NWSL club," Associated Press. January 14, 2013.

Vecsey, George. "American Resilience a Reflection of Coach's Freewheeling Style," *New York Times*. August 22, 2008

Whiteside, Kelly. "Wambach Leaps into Olympic Fray," *USA Today*. July 25, 2012.

Websites

Cartell, Sean "SEC Soccer at 20: Abby Wambach," SEC Digital Network. November 3, 2012. http://www.secdigitalnetwork.com/NEWS/tabid/473/Article/238697/sec-soccer-at-20-abby-wambach.aspx.

"History of Rochester, New York," Your Rochester Hometown http://www.yourrochesterrealtor.com/welcome-to-rochester/our-history/

Abby Wambach Official Site
http://abbywambach.com

U.S. Soccer
http://www.ussoccer.com

U.S. Youth Soccer Association
http://www.usyouthsoccer.org/

INDEX